How to Become a Better Leader

Essential Leadership Qualities to Bring Out the Best In You and Your Staff

By: Betty Adams

9781635012712

I0510863

PUBLISHERS NOTES

Disclaimer – Speedy Publishing LLC

Speedy Publishing LLC

40 E Main Street, Newark, Delaware, 19711

Contact Us: 1-888-248-4521

Website: http://www.speedypublishing.co

REPRINTED Paperback Edition: 9781635012712:

Manufactured in the United States of America

DEDICATION

This book is dedicated to my partner in crime and in life, Sandra. We may not have the best of all relationships but it's surely worth the fight..

TABLE OF CONTENTS

Chapter 1 - The Two Sides of Leadership: The Dark and the Light

Napoleon once said: "One bad general does better than two good ones." It takes a moment for the sense of this to register, but it is the same as our modern saying that "too many cooks spoil the broth". Having one set of instructions, even if they are flawed, is preferable to having two sets of perfect directions that, when enacted together without reference to each other, cause havoc.

This is the principle of leadership in a nutshell. It is all about maintaining focus and creating positive outcomes.

The same can be applied to individuals who strive to become leaders. There needs to be focus and determination. Advice can be given, but does not have to be heeded. History is full of leaders whose beginnings were disastrous, and had they listened to the naysayers of this world, the world would be a poorer place today.

Leadership can be learned. Some people are certainly born with leadership skills, but this is not a prerequisite for becoming a leader. More important is dedication to the art of leadership. Leadership involves understanding how to inspire, influence and control how people behave. It is not a simple matter of shouting, or having a deep and booming voice; or being great in physical stature; Gandhi possessed none of these attributes, but managed to lead a nation and inspire millions around the world.

Sometimes, leadership may be no more than having a poignant message for a receptive audience at an opportune moment. Of itself, leadership is neither good nor bad; the world has known more than its fair share of evil and charismatic dictators.

In the world of business, the perception of leadership has changed from its early days when it largely mirrored the military model of leadership from the top down, with powerful individuals dominating large groups of less powerful people.

Nowadays, leadership in business is far more knowledge-driven. The lowliest employee may end up effectively leading the direction of a vast corporation through his or her innovative ideas. Anyone with critical knowledge can show leadership. This is known as thought-leadership. In other situations, leadership can be about taking a stand for what you believe in, and trying to convince people to think and act differently.

Leadership has been variously described as the "process of social influence in which one person can enlist the aid and support of others in the accomplishment of a common task"; "creating a way for people to contribute to making something extraordinary happen"; "the ability to successfully integrate and maximize available resources within the internal and external environment for the attainment of organizational or societal goals"; and "the capacity of leaders to listen and observe, to use their expertise as a starting point to encourage dialogue between all levels of decision-making, to establish processes and transparency in decision-making, to articulate their own values and visions clearly but not impose them. Leadership is about setting and not just reacting to agendas, identifying problems, and initiating change that makes for substantive improvement rather than managing change".

There is truth to all of the above definitions, but they all apply to the ideals of leadership.

So what of leadership gone awry?

The Leader Types That You Should Not Become

The dark side of any individual when allowed to go unchecked can create a rigid and dysfunctional personality that stifles creativity, and taints or ruins relationships. When such characteristics are given reign in a leader, a self-righteous and bombastic person can result, who alienates the very people they are meant to inspire.

The Compulsive Leader

Compulsive leaders feel like they have to do everything themselves. They try to manage every aspect of their business, often refusing to delegate, and cannot resist having their say on everything. As they lack trust in others, they cannot let anyone else take responsibility, therefore they restrict personal growth in their team.

Compulsive leaders have many other traits. They are perfectionists who must follow highly rigid and systematized daily routines, and are concerned with status. Thus they strive to impress their superiors with their diligence and efficiency and continually look for reassurance and approval. This can lead to them becoming workaholics, and their team is viewed as failing if they don't keep pace. Spontaneity is not encouraged as this bucks the routine.

Despite this appearance of total control, such leaders can be fit to explode on the inside, and this can be the result of a childhood environment where unrealistic expectations were placed on them. Their attempts to keep control are linked to their attempts to suppress anger and resentment, which makes them susceptible to outbursts of temper if they perceive they are losing their grip.

The Narcissistic Leader

Narcissistic leaders are focused on themselves. Life and the world revolve around them, and they must be at the center of all that is happening. Whilst they exaggerate their own merits, they will try to ignore the merits of others, or seek to devalue them, because other people's accomplishments are seen as a threat to their own standing. The worst type of narcissistic leader cannot tolerate even a hint of criticism and disagreement, and avoid their self-delusions and fantasies being undermined by surrounding themselves with sycophants.

Where possible, they will attempt to use the merits of others for their own advancement, and think nothing of stepping on people to get ahead. Their own feeling of self-importance means they are unable to empathize with those in their team, because they cannot feel any connection. Their only focus is on receiving plaudits that further bolster their sense of greatness. Such an attitude is often the result of a deep-seated inferiority complex, and thus no matter how much they are achieving, they will never feel it is enough.

Some narcissistic leaders take on a sidekick, but this person is expected to toe the line at all times, and serves only to reflect glory onto them and loudly approve of all that they do. Clever sidekicks can subtly manipulate the leader into focusing on the operational outcome of their plans, rather than just their own self-aggrandizement. Ultimately, this type of leader can be very successful if their vision is strong and they get the organization to identify with them and think like they do. Such productive narcissists have more perspective, and can step back and even laugh at their own irrational needs.

The Paranoid Leader

Paranoid leaders are exactly as they sound: paranoid that other people are better than they are, and thus they view even the mildest criticism as devastating. They are liable to overreact if they sense they are being attacked, especially in front of other people. This can manifest itself in open hostility.

This attitude is the result of an inferiority complex that perceives even the most constructive criticism in the wrong way. The paranoid leader will be guarded in their dealings with other people because they do not want to reveal too much of themselves in case they display their weaknesses and are attacked or undermined. They may be scared that their position is undeserved, therefore can be deeply suspicious of colleagues who may steal their limelight or perhaps challenge for their position.

This is not always a wholly negative trait, however. A healthy dose of paranoia may be the secret to success in business, because it helps keep leaders on their toes, always aware of opportunities not to be missed. It is the opposite end of the spectrum to being complacent, and can make for a very successful venture.

The Codependent Leader

Co-dependent leaders do not enjoy taking the lead, and instead seek to copy what others have done or are doing. They avoid confrontation and would rather cover up problems than face them head-on. Planning ahead is not their forte. They tend instead to react to whatever it will be that comes their way, rather than acting to alter outcomes or achieve goals. Codependent leaders, therefore, are not leaders at all. They are reactionary and have the habit of keeping important information to themselves because they are not prepared to act upon it. This can clearly lead to poor outcomes because all the pertinent facts are not known to those below the leader who may be charged with making decisions.

This type of leader avoids confrontation and is thus liable to accept a greater workload rather than respond negatively to any request. They are also prone to accepting the blame for situations they have not caused.

The Passive-Aggressive Leader

Passive-aggressive leaders feel like they need to control everything, and when they can't they cause problems for those who are in control. However, they are sneaky in their ploys, and are very difficult to catch out. Their main characteristics are that they can be stubborn, purposely forgetful, intentionally inefficient, complaining (behind closed doors), and they parry demands put on them through procrastination.

Typically, if they feel they are not firmly in the driving seat, they will jump out and puncture the tires when no one is looking, then feign horror and pretend to search around for a tire iron. This type of leader has two speeds: full speed ahead and stopped. When situations do not go their way, they will offer their full support for whatever has been decided, then gossip and back stab, willfully cause delays, and generally create upset. When confronted, they claim to have been misinterpreted. Passive aggressive leader are often chronically late for appointments, using any excuse to dominate and regain some control of the situation.

Dealing with passive-aggressive leaders is thus a draining and frustrating affair that saps energy. They are not averse to short outbursts of sadness or anger to regain some control, but are ultimately fearful of success since it leads to higher expectations.

Chapter 2- Effective Leaders Lead by Influence

Leading people has nothing to do with managing them. Too many managers are trying to micro-manage their staff, all the while forgetting to lead them effectively.

If you want to become a strong leader you need to lead by example. This means you have to show your team that you are perfectly capable to set examples. By doing, so you will earn their respect and create lifelong devotees who would move mountains to please you.

Conversely, a manager who hides behind his office door while his staff does all the work isn't going to gain much respect in the work place.

Ultimately the success of any business venture lies in the hands of its employees and NOT the managers. A manager's responsibility is to organize and manage business systems, systems that will see to the successful finalization of projects.

If your staffs are unhappy it will soon show in their lack of productivity. This will influence your bottom line. Chances are customer complaints will start to amass and office gossip will run hot. This is counterproductive to running a well-oiled machine – your business.

Build Bridges, Not Burn Them

No organization can function for very long without the co-operation of its employees. Unfortunately, the necessity in any organization is that there are various levels of status within the team, and this can lead to conflicts if not managed properly.

The effective leader has to realize that the team under them is there because they have to be. Most employees work to earn money, not because they enjoy the daily grind of a nine-to-five.

For this reason, there must be an effort to build healthy relationships, or life in the workplace can become untenable for everyone, and productivity will decline.

Leaders need to make their workplace society function positively, with co-operation and respect. In this way everyone is working for the common good and towards a common purpose. This demands that effective relationships are built upon an understanding of each other's needs. It is no different to how things should be in the home; no personal relationship will last very long if there is a sense that one or both parties are being selfish.

The most effective way to understand how other people are feeling is to listen to what they have to say. This must be done without judging, and not as though you are being forced to do so by some higher authority. Very often, teams will have the same goals as their leaders, but may just want to know that they are not seen as automatons that have no creative input. Quality workplace relationships make people feel happy. One of the major reasons why employees move on from a company is because of relationship clashes with leaders or other colleagues.

Leaders should also make sure that they create the circumstances for understanding within their team, and this means asking questions. Assuming that your team will simply pipe up and express their feelings is not enough; many people will not feel it is their place to speak up unless they are specifically asked to do so.

Listening should be done attentively, not glancing at your watch every couple of minutes or trying not to look bored. This means you listen without interrupting or fidgeting, and with the correct expression. Your expression, by the way, should be genuine or you will be found out very quickly and the situation will become worse than had you not asked in the first place. A great way to foster healthy relationships with your team is by meeting them in a more social environment on regular occasions. Some companies choose to send their staff to regular golfing outings while others prefer to host a monthly BBQ or weekend trips.

Regardless what you end up choosing, the key lies in giving your team a chance to connect away from the daily grind.

Building effective relationships means that neither party must make any assumptions. As a leader, you cannot expect people to understand exactly what we want and why you want it. Sometimes it is this lack of comprehension that causes problems. As much as you must trust your team members to have intelligence, if they are not party to the goals you are working towards they can become resistant. As far as possible, your team should be conversant with your goals and how their actions are contributing to their successful outcome. Humans are inquisitive and function better when not kept in the dark.

Respect is the key ingredient of any good relationship, and this means respect for yourself as well as others. Genuinely listening and understanding are the ways in which you show that you respect the person you are talking to. Quickly judging based on preconceived ideas or prejudice is the opposite of having respect. Bear in mind that not everyone will respond in 100% perfect fashion to all that occurs in the workplace. Although it is not the leader's job to be a permanent shoulder to cry on, it is important to accept that your team is made up of individuals whose lives may not be as perfect as their coffee-break banter might lead you to believe.

Whilst creating a healthy working relationship is a crucial goal, the smart leader will always bear in mind that conflict is inevitable and must be managed, rather than ignored for the sake of apparent peace.

Relationships can never improve unless problems are identified and confronted. Differences between people are inevitable, and hearing them aired can lead to some very useful resolutions that produce ideas beyond the expected. The alternative is highly detrimental: to let problems fester and build, and ruin the atmosphere in a workplace, if not productivity levels.

Keys for success in working relationships:

1. One party at least should value the relationship – This may start off as a one-way street, but this can lead to a meeting of minds later on.

2. Listen effectively, without judging – Listening in this way will promote mutual understanding and mutual respect.

3. Have informal chats – Chatting over a coffee can encourage a more frank exchange of views than meeting officially with a desk between you.

4. Create an open culture – Your team should know they can speak freely, no matter if that is to express happiness, joy, contentment, anger, irritation, sadness or fear. Negative feelings that are hoarded cause significant problems.

Changing Minds by Empowering Employees

Leaders must take responsibility for their team's performance, which means leaders must be happy that the direction of their team is one which the leader thinks is best. Although it is useful to have creative sessions with team members to bat around a few ideas, the overarching goals that the team must fulfill are most often set by the leader, or some authority above the leader.

The challenge is therefore to get the team "onside" with the given aims, even when some team members may wholeheartedly disagree with them, or baulk at the idea that these have been imposed on them from above.

Despite the accepted hierarchy of any workplace, for a team to work most efficiently, its members – especially higher level ones – may want to feel they are contributing more than the spade work; they may like to feel that they have chosen where some of the plots should be dug.

This presents a challenge for the leader who cannot just let his or her subordinates have free play. The team must be made to feel involved and motivated. Or perhaps the situation is worse, and your team is beginning to show a little disobedience. How then to provoke a positive response in them?

The answer is by empowering your team, as far as possible. Short of handing over the reins and heading off home, the motivational leader must be able to create a sense that their team is actively involved in the process and contributing in a real sense to the overall outcome of the project. This can involve learning how to make your suggestions appeal to them. This may mean you solicit their opinions and take the best ideas on board. Or you may have to convince them that your goals are shared and that their futures are tied to your overall success. It may be a simple matter of making an employee understand that their job will be safer if they perform well; reminding them that they are working for themselves and their family, and not just for a company.

However, empowering others does not just mean employing tactics that persuade other people to your own opinion or goals. It can also mean demonstrating leadership qualities that inspire others to act at their very best, no matter what is asked of them. Such leadership qualities would be most in evidence in the armed services, where the end result of potentially being killed is rarely going to elicit a whoop and a cheer. Soldiers are empowered to greatness by the examples set by their commanding officers.

Sometimes, it is just a matter of being an admirable and inspirational human being. Of course, some are born with more of these qualities than others, but we can all strive to lead by example, so that others will feel empowered to make great things happen.

Chapter 3- A Leader's Take On Conflict and Stress in the Workplace

Many different things and factor can motivate a person in the workplace, but there are also different factors that can also motivate conflict and inflict stress in the workplace. One key factor is stress management, how the person handles stress is what will make or break a working relationship.

There are three main key theories that suggest how people reacts and pushes people to have the initiative or motivation or drive to do their job well and better while also relieving stress on the workplace.

Before we tackle the different theories of motivating employees in the workplace, let's find out why is it important to emphasize and create a process of motivation.

Any organizations flourish with employees. It's the most important part for any organizations. Without them, there's is no one to do the selling. Managers have been long known to think creative ways to keep employees motivated and hard working. Making sure they come to work regularly and energetic and continuously providing work that are positive contributions for the company. When they are so, the business will be able to save up and cut costs while able to make more profit, which is the goal of any business or organizations built. Unmotivated employees are what you can say a bit of a challenge to handle. Though they are qualified to their work, they are less likely to work on it. They are not willing to do well in their jobs or sometimes organizations will even require hiring other people to do different jobs that sadly results to high operating costs and reduction on profit which are not in favor for the company as well as the employees.

According to an article entitled „Need-based Perspectives on Motivation" by Moorhead and Griffin, job performance depends on three main factors: Motivation, Ability and Environment. In order for an employee to reach a higher level of performance, he/she must „want to do the job" (motivation), „be able to do the job" (ability), and „must have the materials, resources, and equipment to do the job" (environment).

"Performance = Motivation + Ability + Environment"

As stated above, within those three factors, motivation is simply the hardest and most difficult factor to manage and apply. This is basically due to the fact that a person's attitude and behavior are simply too complicated. It's filled with complexities and fallacies thus making it hard to categorize and to manage. While the other two factors – Ability and Environment – are things that employee understands that he/she has been recruited for and has the awareness that he/she has the skills and capacity needed to perform the tasks as well as the fact that resources are readily available and if a manager sees that an employee lacks certain aspects of the job, he or she can provide training programs to learn that particular skill to be more efficient for the company.

If, however, an employee isn't suitable for the job or lacks hereof, the knowledge and ability for the job, there are other jobs that he/she can do, but if other resources are not available (the environment factor) the manager can take action to ensure that they become available.

For example, if an employee needs a photocopier, he/she can formulate request to the management team and ask for one. For this reason, it is quite clear that the most challenging job for every employer is how to motivate their employees to strive their best to work for the organization.

But if other resources are not available (the environment factor) the manager can take action to ensure that they become available. For example, if an employee needs a photocopier, he/she can formulate request to the management team and ask for one. For this reason, it is quite clear that the most challenging job for every employer is how to motivate their employees to strive their best to work for the organization.

Intrinsic Motivation Theory

Intrinsic Motivation Theory is used by "management teams" to motivate people with intrinsic rewards. Under this theory employees desire to do a good job because they are proud of what they are doing, and want to be a part of something good. For example, a Disney Imaginer feels satisfaction when he or she creates a new ride. The feeling of being a part of something so spectacular motivates him or her to do a great job.

Theory of Scientific Management

The Theory of Scientific Management has a unique view on how workers are motivated. It suggests that workers are motivated by what they produce, on their productivity while Intrinsic Theory suggests that they are motivated to do a great satisfying job. It states that workers aims to produce a lot of products in a specific period of time. To put it simply, workers are paid more if they are more productive. This theory is often used for businesses since they require high productivity and mass production. However, overuse of this theory also conclude that employees will soon feel they are machines rather than co-workers which in turn result to dissatisfaction which is why the Intrinsic theory promotes a happier workplace than the Scientific Management Theory.

The Goal Setting Theory

Another theory is the Goal Setting Theory wherein as stated and developed both by Lotham and Locke in the year 1979 that a certain level of motivation and performance is higher when the individual has specific objectives established and when these objectives, even with a high level of difficulty, are accepted and are offered performance feedback. The employees must participate in the process of goal setting in order to obtain their approval when setting higher and higher targets and the human resources people can help them to understand the consequences of these targets over their entire activity. Feedback is also vital to maintain the employee's motivation, especially when targeting even higher objectives.

Motivation-Hygiene Theory

Similar to the Intrinsic Theory, the Motivation-Hygiene Theory suggests motivation through pride but rather than result-oriented, this theory states about employees pride through proper hygiene and appearance. Though this theory is still not completely proven to motivate employees, how they look and how they manage their hygiene it is, in fact, helps increase self-esteem that does help for better performance. The best motivator though is the pride an employee takes in a job well done.

Employees that are too stressed out create output with lower quality and productivity. Stress can also result to illness which can either be physical, like fatigue, or mental like anxiety and tension. However, a certain amount of stress is required to keep employees motivated. If things run too smoothly, employees can become inattentive and bored to do their work.

Adams" Equity Theory

Categorized as one of the "justice" theories, The Equity Theory which was first developed and studied by John Stacey Adams claims and states that through satisfying the needs of fairness and equality brought upon by managers are a drive that brings out the best results from his/her employees. Equity theory places value on fair treatment.

An individual will consider that he is treated fairly when he feels that the he receives the amount similar to his output and it is the same to other people around him. In this case, it would be acceptable for an employee who has much more work experience and who is a more senior colleague to receive higher compensation/salary for his/her job.

However, if an employee feels that another individual who is as skillful as him and provides the same effort and output but earning more recognition or compensation, he will feel he's treated unfairly and thus perform at a lower level on his tasks.

An employee who feels he is over-compensated may increase his effort, but, he may also change the perceptions of his inputs and feel a sense of superiority, which may lead to him decreasing his efforts instead.

The Expectancy Theory

In this theory, both Maslow's and Herzberg's motivation theories presents that motivations is triggered by expectations. Though this is true in some points, by generalizing it both theories are criticized. It is obvious with many other recent researches that „the same people are motivated by different things at different times and that different people are motivated by different things at the same time. Therefore, there is no certain category of motivation. "Expectancy" refers to the "subjective probability" that one thing will result in another. Individual perception is, therefore, an essential part of Expectancy theory.

With this theory, an expectancy model was designed and here determined that one's motivation is strengthened as their perceived effort-performance and performance-reward probabilities increase. It may seem quite complicated, but we can discuss it through examples.

For instance, how strong can you be motivated to study if you expect to score poorly on your tests no matter how hard you study (low effort-performance probability) and when you know that the tests will not be graded (low performance-reward probability)? In contrast, your motivation to study will increase if you know that u can score well on the tests with just a little hard work (high effort-performance probability) and that your grades will be significantly improved (high performance-reward probability).

Employees and staffs are no different from students or any other people. They are simply motivated to do and work harder if it will give them better and more valuable rewards.

With this, an employee's contribution is determined on their rewards expectation. With this said, managers and leaders can create strategies to try to push them to work harder by making favorable expectations for their employees. When people can expect personally valued rewards, they will undoubtedly work harder to try to accomplish their tasks.

This is where one qualities of managers must have that will help; listening. One must listen to his/her employees, remember what they experienced as an employee and discover what rewards certain employees" value. So the manager can potentially enhance their employees" willingness to put more efforts into their work.

CHAPTER 4- USING THE THEORIES OF MOTIVATION IN ACTION

From theory to actual practice, motivation strategies are important. Though, applying which theory to use is quite tricky, however, practicing each varies depending on its application and to whom you are applying it with, in this case the employees.

Do they respond to praises and appreciations? Do they tend to respond on relaxed hours and a relaxed dress code? To structure and advertised perks related to performance?

Try understanding each theory by applying it to the workplace. You can try testing them all out and see which theory best works for the workplace and the employees within it.

A Just and Effective Reward System Encourages Employee Retention

Rewards are a great way to reinforce motivation in an employee's behavior and productivity. A reward is a work outcome of positive value to the individual. It's common for many organizations and companies to have a reward system given to those employees who exerts excellent performances, accomplishing great deals that are proving worth for the company's ideals. There are two types of reward system.

Extrinsic rewards are rewards and motivators that are received "externally". These are rewards given to employees when one's outcomes are perceived as great and best and usually given by managers or supervisors. Examples of extrinsic rewards are pay bonuses, promotions, time off, special assignments, office fixtures, awards, verbal praise, and so on. In all cases, the motivational stimulus of extrinsic rewards originates outside the individual.

Intrinsic rewards are something that comes from the "inside". These are rewards that make a person feel "special" or "high" after completing a job. That person feels good because she has a feeling of competency, personal development, and self-control over her work. In comparison with extrinsic rewards, intrinsic is compelled not by actions of other people.

Killing Burnout through Job Redesign

Though jobs and employment are important, people who goes to their work every day doing the same thing makes the job seems mundane and boring. According to some individuals who experience this called it as "burnout". This is common to any company either small or large companies, but a smart manager can handle this situation if he knows what he's going to do.

The concept of job redesign, which requires understanding for the human qualities people bring with them to the organization, applies motivational theories to the structure of work for improving productivity and satisfaction.

When redesigning jobs, managers look at both job scope and job depth. Redesign attempts may include the following:

Setting Up Varieties of Tasks per Employee

Job enlargement isn't adding more tasks but simply setting up lists of varieties of tasks that are included in their employment. It doesn't increase the job nor the quality and even the difficulty but instead decreases boredom and monotony of the tasks at hand. With this, it helps decrease inactivity and increase work quality of productivity.

How an Organization Benefits from a Cross-Trained Workforce

This method allows people to experience different tasks in the company. This is, however, not permanent but rather allows employees to be exposed on the company's other jobs and also add variety and decrease boredom on employees. Job rotation can encourage higher levels of contributions and renew interest and enthusiasm. The organization benefits from a cross-trained workforce.

Enriching Lives One Job at a Time

This is also called vertical job loading but beside adding or giving a variety of tasks to an employee it also includes added responsibility and more authority. If the skills required to do the job are skills that match the jobholder's abilities, job enrichment may improve morale and performance.

Flexibility Encourages Productivity

Personal Time: Employees also requires this and fights for it. They need for many reasons such as family time and emergencies. The traditional nine-to-five workday may not work for many people anymore. That's why give "flextime". This gives employees the choice to set and control their own working hours. It's a sure method for any companies to be accommodating to his employees. Here are some other options organizations are trying as well:

A compressed workweek is a form of flextime that allows a fulltime job to be completed in less than the standard 40-hour, five-day workweek. Its most common form is the 4/40 schedule, which gives employees three days off each week. This schedule benefits the individual through more leisure time and lower commuting costs. The organization should benefit through lower absenteeism and improved performance. Of course, the danger in this type of scheduling is the possibility of increased fatigue.

Job sharing or twinning occurs when one fulltime job is split between two or more persons. This often happens when there are employees working for half day, but it can also be done on weekly or monthly depending on sharing arrangements decided. When jobs can be split and shared, organizations can benefit by employing talented people who would otherwise be unable to work fulltime. For example, parents or mothers who need to take care of their children or their elders that are willing to work half-day. Although adjustment problems sometimes occur, the arrangement can be good for all concerned.

Telecommuting, sometimes called "flexiplace", is a work-arrangement that allows at least a portion of scheduled work hours to be completed outside of the office, with work-at-home as one of the options. Telecommuting frees the jobholder from needing to work fixed hours, wearing special work attire, enduring the normal constraints of commuting, and having direct contact with supervisors. Home workers often demonstrate increased productivity, report fewer distractions, enjoy the freedom to be their own boss, and appreciate the benefit of having more time for them.

Of course, when there are positives, there are also negatives. Many home workers feel that they work too much and are isolated from their family and friends. In addition to the feelings of isolation, many employees feel that the lack of visibility at the office may result in the loss of promotions.

There is no limit and different factors on how to motivate your employees on the workplace. A manager's responsibility is to understand his employees' needs and find effective ways to relieve their stress and make their daily working lives more relaxed and comfortable. All of these things will make for a pleasant and more productive workplace.

CHAPTER 5- A GOOD LEADER ENCOURAGES EMPLOYEE PARTICIPATION AT ALL TIMES

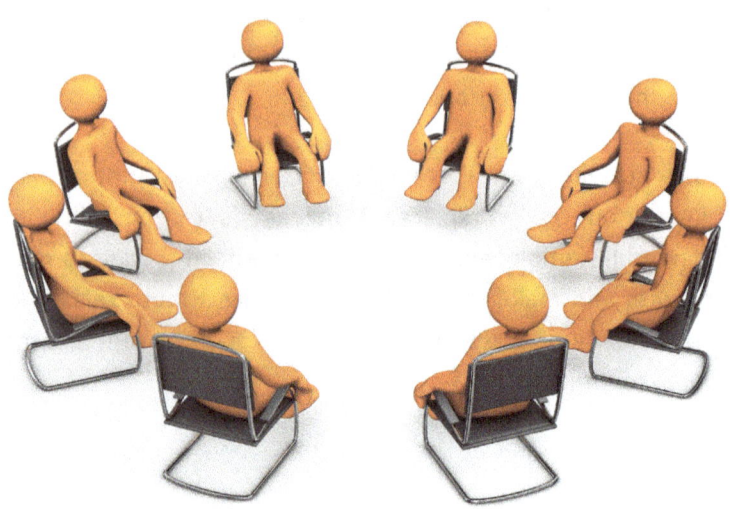

Put yourself on your employee's shoes, or just remember the time when you're not the manager. When your work isn't noticed or appreciated you feel that you're just a disposable employee of the company wherein they can replace you anytime.

If that's the case, then that's a workplace you'll definitely want to leave anytime.

This is not the type of working environment we or any managers want to implement and encourage on the workplace since the main goal is to motivate and retain professional employees and them providing excellent results. So, as managers, one of your main responsibilities is creating a positive working environment wherein your employees will feel valued and appreciated. An environment wherein they can feel they are needed and contributing to the success of the company.

In today's modern employment system, you can easily find new employees either fresh graduates or professionals, however, getting them working while being involve for the benefit of both the company or organization and themselves can be quite a difficult task. That said, when an employee feel that he/she is contributing to the welfare of the company or business, they are likely happier with their position and will stay loyal and to the company and producing more and higher quality of work.

Creating change to employee initiative and motivation can be quite hard especially when your employees have already settled down with the environment and the system the company uses. Shifts in marketing and sales strategy, management structure, workplace technologies or other areas can alter a business drastically.

Changes in the company whether small or fundamental may change how your employees will handle their responsibilities requiring them in some cases to learn new skills to remain productive. Change can also add stress. Psychological stress can build up as employees and staff must compromise and adjust to the changes and meet the needs of the company. For all these reasons, it's vital to inspire employees to work for change rather than against it.

Studies show that high-involvement work practices can develop the positive beliefs and attitudes associated with employee engagement. These practices also show that it also generates different kinds of discretionary behaviors that lead to enhanced performance. Simply put, employees who conceive the design and implement workplace and process changes are engaged employees.

Employee involvement is crucial in motivating them while creating an environment wherein people have an impact on decisions and actions that affect their jobs.

However, getting employee involvement isn't a goal or a tool for companies and organizations but rather a philosophy. It's leadership and management philosophy on how people respond and contribute to continuous improvement and the ongoing success of their work organization.

It can be critically important to competitiveness in the contemporary business environment. Employee engagement was positively associated with performance in a variety of areas, including increased customer satisfaction, profitability and productivity, and reduced employee turnover. The breadth of employee involvement was substantial. About 2/3 of the business units scoring above the median on employee engagement also scored above the median on performance, while only about 1/3 of companies below the median on employee involvement scored above the median on performance (Harter, Schmidt & Hayes, 2002).

There are 3 main related components when it comes to employee involvement: a cognitive, an emotional, and a behavioral aspect.

Cognitive Aspect –concerns employees" beliefs about the organization, its leaders, and working conditions.

Emotional Aspect – concerns how employees feel about each of those three factors and whether they have positive or negative attitudes toward the organization and its leaders.

Behavioral Aspect – concerns about the value-added component for the organization and consists of the discretionary effort engaged employees bring to their work in the form of extra time, brainpower and energy devoted to the task and the firm.

Getting employees to be involved when it comes to the company's welfare such as decision making is important to continue the improvement and success of the business. Using strategic methods like employees suggestion systems, manufacturing cells, work teams and events you can employ involvement into employees. Other methods can include Kaizen (continuous improvement) events, corrective action processes, and periodic discussions with the supervisor.

Being good in business calls on being good at being human," Petzinger concludes after studying the turnaround of Rowe Furniture Company. Rowe, which had been a very traditional manufacturing company, identified the need to utilize the brains and talent of its employees. Charlene Pedrolie, its manufacturing chief, truly believed that the people doing the work should design how the work is done.

With the assistance and consultation from a much reduced management team and engineers, workers redesigned their work. They moved from an environment in which each person handled part of a work process to fully cross-trained manufacturing cells producing a whole product.

From standing at an assembly position all day long, they created work which allowed some freedom and movement. They eliminated the formerly "deadly dull" jobs. At the same time, the flow of information they received, which allowed them to know exactly how they were performing, increased dramatically.

The new sense of personal control, according to Petzinger, "bred a culture of innovation in every corner of the planet..." It reveals the creative power of human interaction. It suggests that efficiency is intrinsic; that people are naturally productive; that when inspired with vision, equipped with the right tools, and guided by information about their performance, people will build on each other's action to a more efficient result than any single brain could design.

Employee Involvement Model

As mentioned, there are different methods to apply to instill employee involvement. Different models can be used. One of the best tried, and tested model was developed from research theories from Tannenbaum and Schmidt (1958) and Sadler (1970). They suggest that through continuous proper leadership plus involvement increases the chance of employees motivations making them take more roles willingly and decrease role of supervisors with the decision process.

Tell: the supervisor makes the decision and announces it to staff. The supervisor provides complete direction. Example: Useful when communicating about safety issues, government regulations, decisions that neither require nor ask for employee input.

Sell: the supervisor makes the decision and then attempts to gain commitment from staff by "selling" the positive aspects of the decision.

Example: Useful when employee commitment is needed, but the decision is not open to employee influence.

Consult: the supervisor invites input into a decision while retaining authority to make the final decision herself.

The key to a successful consultation is to inform employees, on the front end of the discussion, that their input is needed but that the supervisor is retaining the authority to make the final decision. This is the level of involvement that can create employee dissatisfaction most readily when this is not clear to the people providing input.

Join: the supervisor invites employees to make the decision with the supervisor. The supervisor considers her voice equal in the decision process.

The key to a successful join is when the supervisor truly builds consensus around a decision and is willing to keep her influence equal to that of the others providing input.

Delegate: the supervisor turns the decision over to another party.

Chapter 6- Are You A Born Leader? How Genetics Dictate Your Leadership Style

The matter on leadership and genetics has been discussed and researched on for as long as the concept of leadership was created. Research efforts have been poured into exploring the link between the two. Are leaders born or made? This is going to sound cliché but until now, genetics is still considered a big factor in determining the formation of leaders. But not everyone thinks the same way. There could be some truth to it but factors such as experiences and social dynamics are also important in leadership. There is no single factor that will determine the person's ability to lead. Each factor is important up to a certain extent.

Some scientists feel strongly about genetic and biological factors and their link with leadership. The interest in the link between genetics and leadership are sparked by people from the same family that assume leadership positions in society. The Kennedys and the Bush family are two examples. More than genetics, science is also looking at biological and physical traits that leaders possess. There are studies that show how genetics contribute to the physiological and psychological functions of a person. These will eventually affect the person's cognitive and behavioral traits, which determine if the person is fit for leadership. Hormones and chemical changes in the body affect a person's cognitive functioning, a very important aspect of leadership.

When it comes to leadership, it's always a question about nature vs. nature. However, both are intertwined with each other and cannot be separated. Leadership cannot be discussed without considering both at the same time. Case in point would be chemical and hormonal changes in the body that will affect the disposition of the person. The disposition will affect the attitude and behavior, which are huge factors in leadership.

An example would be a person that is suffering from a bipolar disorder. People with bipolar disorder tend to exhibit very drastic mood swings, easily switching from euphoria to depression. There are several causes of bipolar disorder, including neurotransmitters that are hereditary. Their bipolar tendencies will affect their personality, which will affect their leadership style. This is not to say that bipolar people are not capable leaders. In fact, the greatest leaders in the world were reportedly bipolar (e.g. Abraham Lincoln, Winston Churchill, and Napoleon Bonaparte). Their drastic mood swings, however, may have negative effects on their leadership and establishing trust with their followers.

As said earlier, you cannot rule out the external factors (nurture) in leadership. The Kennedys may be a family of leaders but take note that the members are exposed to the same environment and values. They are exposed to almost the same group of people and circumstances. Even if genetics played a big part in their leadership streak, you cannot take away the fact that they thrive in a common environment. They were exposed to the same kind of experiences and brought up by the same set of people who share the same values as well. They are also bound to develop similar opinions on important issues and perhaps, develop the same leadership style.

There are certain environments that are conducive for molding leaders. The environment plays a huge role in shaping the ideals, opinions, and values of a person. If young children are brought up by parents that promote pro-social behavior, the children will grow up overcoming unreasonable aggression and form healthy relationships with their peers. Role models account a lot for the formation of leadership traits in a person. When a child is surrounded by people with strong leadership attributes, the child will most likely imbibe these attributes as well. Likewise, children surrounded with aggressive role models will most likely turn out to be aggressive. Aggression and social skills are very important in leadership because to be an effective leader, the individual must be adept in dealing with people. Leaders have to establish rapport with their colleagues and subordinates.

In general, many leadership attributes are shaped by external factors. Even if there are claims that leadership qualities are inherent in a person, the fact remains that a person will continue to develop for as long as he or she is alive. Some traits will be more developed by others. The attitude and personality of the person will be influenced by the people around him or her. Other environmental factors that affect the person (e.g. political atmosphere, economic conditions, and life-changing events) will also determine the set of leadership traits he or she will possess. Such are the formative experiences that can possibly produce a leader.

Related to the formative experiences are the social dynamics that the person is subject to. For instance, a certain female may have good social-skills and strong conviction but her leadership qualities may not shine to its full potential if she is in a society where males are always considered the alpha figure. She may have the leadership potential but if she thinks that males are always the rightful leader, she will not be able to exhibit her leadership qualities to their fullest. The position in the family is also an example of the impact of social dynamics on leadership. Many first-borns are usually molded to become leaders, although not all turn out to be good leaders.

Social dynamics are huge factors to a certain extent, similar to genetics and formative experiences. All three contribute to the development of a leader. Some people may or may not have inherent leadership qualities but experiences and relationships in life will affect the attitude of the person. Leadership qualities may be enhanced along the way. One's growth and development is certainly crucial in determining of the person is fit to be a good leader.

Leadership styles vary but surely, there should be common qualities that are common among great leaders. The attributes will gauge if the leader is doing a good job in serving his or her purpose.

Good leaders make a good first impression not because of their skills and achievements. Although these are important, these aren't the first things that their people notice. People are drawn to leaders that are oozing with charisma. Charisma is a very attractive and inspiring trait that many great leaders possess. Identifying charisma is not easy because it cannot be articulated instantly. Charisma is a combination of many things – the way a person stands, moves, speaks, etc. Charismatic leaders have a vision (which will be discussed later) and the ability to articulate this vision. They should also have the ability to communicate with as many people as possible in an emotional level. Charismatic leaders make other people feel that they are able to relate with their plight, something that's not very easy to do. Some people think that charisma is something that cannot be learned. For them, it is an inherent trait in every person. You either have it or you don't. But modern thinkers beg to disagree with this mindset. They think that people can eventually learn to be charismatic, starting with being courteous, polite, and respectful. The point is to be "likeable" and "relatable" to other people. Charismatic leaders make other people feel that they are able to not only understand their situation, but also relate to it as well. Not all have this ability but some are able to build charisma through age and time.

Leadership requires good people skills and sensitivity to others' needs, also building blocks of charisma. After all, leadership would not exist if there are no people to lead. People skills are built on the small things that people don't forget. For example, they appreciate it when new acquaintances remember their names even if they've only met a few times. Charisma can eventually be developed, as long as the person remembers to make other people feel comfortable and important.

Leadership starts with a focus and vision. Leaders are not required to be all-knowing individuals but they should completely know the purpose and vision of the organization they are spearheading. It is only by having a focus that a solid commitment and responsibility can be formed. Also, a leader must have the competence required in his or her field. Again, he or she need not to be all-knowing but sufficient knowledge in the field is required to make sound judgment calls.

No leader can withstand the challenges of leadership without courage and strength in character. Of all the members in the organization, individuals holding leadership responsibilities cannot be swayed by just anything and anyone. The leader must remember the purpose and vision of the leadership in any decision-making process. The leader must have enough courage to stand up to anything or anyone that threatens to undermine that vision. Good leaders are also assertive in getting the job done and upholding the organization's vision. He or she must be assertive enough to get people to fulfill their duties.

Good leaders should always arm themselves with creativity and resourcefulness because some situations will require them to think outside the box. Not all problems can be solved by textbook formulas and tried-and-tested solutions. They must have enough courage to veer away from the conventional in order to find better ways of doing things.

Finally, a good leader should have loads of passion and a sense of servitude. Leadership is no easy feat and if a leader attempts to fulfill his or her duties devoid of any passion, he or she might not endure the challenges. Leadership is a rollercoaster experience and without passion, the leader might find it difficult to accept the difficulties. As for the sense of servitude, leaders cannot lead if they do not know what it is like to serve. Besides, the leader's purpose is to serve the organization and not just to order people around.

Chapter 7- Gauging The Emotional Intelligence Needed in Leadership

Leadership cannot take place when the leader does not have sufficient emotional intelligence. A leader with enough emotional intelligence can overcome difficult leadership challenges that not a lot of people can fulfill. Studies conducted in the past several years that people with high emotional intelligence are more adept in addressing organizational conflicts more effectively and quickly. Gone are the days when pure intellect was quickly equated with good leadership potential.

Emotional intelligence is a person's ability to acknowledge and deal with his or her own emotions, as well as the emotions of other people. Emotions can fluctuate due to hormonal changes, stress, and unexpected situations that arise but the right amount of emotional intelligence will help the person deal with emotional changes effectively.

People have different personalities, needs, and preferences. Likewise, people have different ways of dealing with situations and expressing their emotions. It takes sound emotional intelligence to deal with different personalities. People may feel different emotions at the same time and more often than not, the challenge is to be able to deal with people's different emotions without sparking conflict and straining relationships. When a person has sufficient emotional intelligence, he or she is able to recognize his or her own emotions and how they affect the people around. Emotional intelligence is also the ability of a person to understand how another person feels. Needless to say, emotional intelligence is needed in managing relationships.

In an organization, the people that stay longer usually have a high emotional intelligence. In fact, high emotional intelligence is more preferred than people with high IQ but with low emotional intelligence. People with high emotional intelligence are easy to work with, compared to those with low emotional intelligence. High emotional intelligence enables people to accomplish things by nurturing good relationships. They can sustain level-headedness even in stressful situations. Emotionally intelligent people are not immune to agitation or stress. However, they can easily get a grip of the situation and look for a solution in the calmest manner possible. Therefore, they are bound to make sound decisions because they manage their emotions well in the decision-making process. Because emotionally intelligent people are level-headed, they don't think too highly or too lowly of themselves. They know their strengths and weaknesses. They utilize their strengths whenever needed but they do not show it off excessively. Likewise, they are humble enough to look at themselves honestly and recognize their weaknesses. Emotionally intelligent people don't succumb to criticism easily. They can take the criticism objectively and use it to enhance their performance.

Emotionally intelligent people are good team players because focus solely on their own success. People with high emotional intelligence look out for the success of the whole group and are willing to modify their own interests and whims for the whole team. They are good empathic listeners with the ability to read people's emotions and feelings. They don't judge right away as well. They try to put themselves in the situation of other people before they come up with a resolution for a conflict in relationships. The attributes mentioned above make emotionally intelligent people good at managing people and relationships.

The Link between Leadership and Emotional Intelligence

Surely, fine abilities and exceptional skills are valuable assets in an organization. It's hard to ignore a person with unabashed brilliance and shining talent. However, the criteria for a good leader go beyond skill and talent. In order to stay in an organization, a person needs a lot of emotional intelligence. This is very true, especially if the person aspires to lead an organization one day. The leader carries a lot of responsibilities that need more than just skill and talent. All the responsibilities attached to leadership can only be carried out well if the leader is equipped with emotional intelligence.

Leadership is a social activity. Leaders need to nurture their emotional intelligence continuously in order to be able to deal with different kinds of personalities in an organization. Emotional intelligence is usually equated with "people skills". Emotional intelligence is not just entirely about people skills, although a lot of emotional intelligence is needed to sharpen one's people skills. Leadership requires forming and maintaining relationships with various personalities. Only a leader with high emotional intelligence can forge solid relationships with his or her team and maintain them. High emotional intelligence will enable a leader to relate with diverse personalities and still motivate each member of the team to meet the organization's goal.

Leadership requires emotional intelligences, especially in times of conflict and pressure. Conflict and problems arise from all sorts of angles. Internal conflict can arise from people in the organization squabbling with each other. To be able to handle such problems, a leader needs emotional intelligence to keep emotions in check. In times of extreme pressure, leaders must be able to avoid explosive outbursts. A good leader should be able put things in perspective instead of succumbing to emotional outbursts. Handling team of diverse personalities is manageable when a leader has the right amount of emotional intelligence. An empathic leader that is considerate to all the members of the team has enough emotional intelligence to confront problematic members of the organization without severing relationships. Emotional intelligence on the side of the leader will enable him or her to help the problematic member to express feelings in a healthy way.

Decision-making is another leadership task that requires immense emotional intelligence. There are going to be many factors affecting a leader's decision, including external factors, critics, and unforeseen situations. A leader with emotional intelligence will have enough level-headedness to weigh the pros and cons of any situation before coming up with a decision. Emotionally-adept leaders have enough capacity to make quick and well-thought of decisions. Leaders need to be emotionally intelligent in order to be independent decision-makers, not swayed by unnecessary factors. It takes emotional intelligence to clearly and objectively look at strengths and weaknesses, especially one's own. Leaders need a good glimpse of their assets and weaknesses in order to come up with a decision and eventually follow-through.

Emotional intelligence can be developed and improved over time. One of the first steps to take would be to practice self-awareness in handling stress. Acknowledging the various emotions felt when under pressure and stress will make it easier to address the issue. By being aware of the various emotions running inside a person's head, the person will easily understand the emotions before the emotions rule over their thoughts, words, and actions. Self-awareness is all about recognizing one's feelings and thoughts but to develop it, you can enlist the help of other people. Seek the feedback of the people around you – supervisors, colleagues, etc. It's also important to get the feedback of other people in order to recognize the impact of your emotions and actions on other people. This is important in enhancing the dynamics and relationship of each member. If the leader can practice self-awareness, he or she can set a good example to the entire team.

Part of self-awareness is knowledge of your strengths and weaknesses. You cannot be too humble to downplay your strengths; this is merely false humility. An emotionally intelligent leader needs to understand that the importance of recognition for efforts without showing off. On the other hand, one cannot be too arrogant with achievements and strengths. A thorough self-evaluation of strengths and weaknesses requires courage and honesty. In relation to self-awareness, you can also start your improving your emotional intelligence by self-reflection. Observe how you react to certain situations, especially the stressful ones. Do you easily burst into a fit? Do you easily snap at your colleagues? These are the things that you need to assess because they are all part of your emotional intelligence.

Improving your emotional intelligence means extending your threshold for stressful situations, whether it be internal conflict in the organization or a big pile of workload. These things really have their way of taking its toll on a person but they're actually things that determine the emotional intelligence of a person. A leader lacking of emotional intelligence will storm away and succumb to these challenges. In the midst of all these challenges, don't just wave your white flag right away. Do not give up on stressful situations without thinking them through. Learn to be aware of your own thoughts when faced with these situations and get a grip of them. Sort out your emotions and distance yourself from them so that you can put things into perspective. Ask yourself, "What can I do and what can't I do?" Look at the problem in terms of the solutions you can provide and let go of the things that have no solutions. Focus your energies on things that can be remedied.

In dealing with problematic colleagues and workers, do not let your emotions lead your decisions and actions. More often than not, a career is usually destroyed because of faulty relationships with co-workers and subordinates. Don't lash out personal tirades against the person. If you have the propensity to blow-up right away, walk away from the problem first and blow off some steam without lashing out at the person. Which part of the problem is the person's fault? Is there anything that could have been done on your part? Are other people involved? Do not focus too much on the person. Instead, address the wrongdoing. When you have put things in perspective, talk to the person but hear out his or her side first. Hear out their viewpoints with no biases, judgments, and stereotypes.

Empathy is very important at this point. It is important as a leader especially when you make decisions concerning your team members involved in the conflict. Even if one of the team members is at fault, it is your job as a leader to ensure that the one at fault will recognize his or her faults without feeling judged. This is a gauge of how much emotional intelligence a leader has.

CHAPTER 8- HOW TO BUILD A STRONG TEAM OF DOERS

If you want to build successful relationships with your people, you have to be able to project yourself as more than just a person with authority. People need to respect you, not fear you. In the previous chapter, empathy and emotional intelligence were discussed lengthily. You are going to need to employ these two in order to establish a stable foundation for your relationships with your team members. It also starts with having a good relationship with yourself. This means getting to know yourself, strengths, weaknesses, potential for improvement, and how you react in various situations. Once you familiarize yourself with your personality, dealing with other people's personalities would be manageable.

Also, part of building a successful relationship with your team is to find out what motivates each one of them so that they can be more productive and ultimately find growth and self-fulfillment for themselves.

One of the leader's duties is to make the whole organization constantly productive. Productivity is undoubtedly important in an organization seeking a competitive and successful edge. Productivity relies on individual and team effort, both of which can be addressed by team building. Team building is supposed to produce a group of individuals that work together to execute different tasks. Trust and strong team dynamics are needed in executing these tasks.

What makes a team strong?

A solid team must have a common goal. A team can be comprised of members performing different functions but they must always have one overriding goal to be able to call themselves one team. The team members are supposed to do their assigned tasks but they should be dependent up to a certain degree on the other members in order to attain the common goal. They will help each other if necessary to realize common goals. Even if they have individual goals, their individual goals must be aligned to the common goals. Cooperation should be ingrained in each team member at all times.

Team building sessions should establish the team goals, recognize issues that hinder the team from achieving those goals, and come up with ways for the whole team to reach those goals. There are guidelines in setting up team building sessions but how each session is designed still depends on the size and nature of the organization. For example, project-based teams usually change in composition constantly. Given these circumstances, team building activities should focus on the skills of each person that will enable him or her to become an effective team member. In a team where membership is relatively permanent, the focus will shift towards how each team member relates with each other. Relationships of the team members with each other will have a direct impact on their productivity. Thus, the nature of the team should be examined before designing a team building session.

The goal of your team building planning should make each team member realize the gravity of their tasks. Each member should also know why they are participating in the organization. By the end of the team building, they should be reminded of their purpose in the organization.

When planning team building activities, make sure that there are activities that are related to the tasks that the people undertake on a normal basis. It does not have to be a completely technical skill but activities that facilitate team dynamics while employing their skills. For example, marketing executives can participate in a team building activity where they are organized in teams and given a certain amount of money to purchase particular things. They have to make the budget fit without compromising the quality of their items and the time constraints. In the end, the participants have to realize that they have to think like their customers. Also, working on this activity in groups will encourage productive brainstorming.

Team building activities should also focus on conflict resolution. Although a chapter will be allotted for this, it is worthwhile to discuss conflict resolution in terms of team building. Different kinds of conflicts will plague the team members and threaten their relationship. Each member must be equipped with the necessary skills in handling conflicts in order to secure a harmonious relationship amongst themselves, their leaders, and the people they deal with on a regular basis.

Conflict is not total bane in an organization. It can facilitate the generation of brilliant ideas and strengthening of relationships, as long as the conflict is handled well.

One of the most sensible ways to manage conflict is to improve the communication lines among members of the organization. You may want to divide your team into pairs and let each pair position themselves back to back. One person should be holding a piece of paper and pencil while the other one holds an image of a shape (definite or abstract). The person holding the picture should describe the shape to the person with the pencil and paper, giving out as much details as possible. The pairs are given a time limit. Once the timer goes off, the pairs are supposed to compare their depiction to the original shape. How did the person with the picture describe the shape? Was it described well? Did the person with the paper and pencil draw the image accurately enough? Were there any communication problems? These are the questions that conflict resolution should tackle.

Conflicts usually stem from the lack of trust, a major team spirit killer. If you are conducting a team building seminar in a huge space, you can perform this activity. To do this, scatter obstacle objects (e.g. cones, chairs, boxes, blocks, tables) around the room. Again, assign the team into pairs. As a leader, take note that this activity is geared towards fixing trust issues. So, you may want to group two people who are having a difficult time trusting each other. Blind fold one person and keep the other person out of the "obstacle area". Put the blindfolded person in the middle of the area and let the other one give instructions to the blindfolded person on how to get out of that area. The blindfolded person cannot talk or speak under any circumstances. The blindfolded person must avoid the obstacles on his or her way out. Let each pair strategize for a few minutes before beginning, but only on how to communicate during the game. Don't let them see the area.

Leaders should facilitate solidarity, even outside team building sessions. As a leader, you should be able to identify if there are any barriers that are hindering people from working together as a team. Some teams, especially the big ones, tend to split into small cliques and teams. Leaders should be able to keep track of these things and recognize the cause, whether petty or serious. Sometimes, the cause can be as petty as different dress codes per department. If this is the cause of conflict, there should be one dress code imposed on all the team members.

This phenomenon is very common in large organizations (e.g. the marketing department getting into a conflict with the human resources department, one branch complaining about the head office, etc.). Leaders with managerial positions would be tempted to host a corporate social function in order to eradicate these boundaries but this plan can backfire if not planned properly. For example, in a casual corporate picnic where all employees are invited, they might still seek their friends and resort to cliques. Worse, this can possibly start a fight since all of the employees are in one venue.

If you want to improve the relationships among members or co-workers, you can start by identifying the barriers or the markers that divide the people before gathering them together in a team building session or a social function. List down the specific conflicts amongst the team and work them out with the people involved. For example, cliques in the office could be caused by language and cultural barriers. FI this is the case, you can occasionally group people of different races for certain tasks.

Encourage transparency and honesty in different but very highly technical departments too. Sometimes, the rift gets bigger when two diverse groups are assigned to work with each other but one of them uses jargon terms when speaking to non-experts. Discourage this attitude from the employees, especially the technical personnel.

Team members are more likely to have strong relationships with each other if they have a good relationship with their leader. While your team is building relationships, guide and monitor them accordingly. Knowing that they have a leader they can consult and who can understand will make them feel secure and confident in forming relationships with their co-members.

Team building is a continuously ongoing process. Determining its success is not done in one sitting. And, any organization that seeks to stay in top shape should always seek to fortify their teams. This cannot be done by just one team building session. In the end, leaders should remember that team building is a long term process. People usually join an organization with the hopes of staying as long as possible, seeking growth and self-fulfillment. With this in mind, the leader should make it a point to establish team building as a continuous and ongoing process. It is futile to set up a teambuilding process only to return to normal activities as if no teambuilding activities ever took place. As time progresses, team building activities should be modified according to the members' competencies, strengths, and weaknesses. Team building activities should be planned in relation to the fruits of previous team building sessions. There should never be an assumption that successful team building does not stop with one session. Organizational teams and relationships need to be nurtured constantly if they are to remain progressive and stable at the same time.

ABOUT THE AUTHOR

Betty owns several companies, thereby having first-hand information on leadership. She holds a Master's Degree in Business Administration.

During her free time, Betty would hold small gatherings with family and friends.

www.ingramcontent.com/pod-product-compliance
Lightning Source LLC
Chambersburg PA
CBHW051249170526
45165CB00004B/1634